Jumping

JACK RUSSELL
TERRIERS

LOYAL! LOVING! SPIRITED!

PERKY! MERRY! DETERMINED!

ABDO
Publishing Company

Pam Scheunemann

Consulting Editor, Diane Craig, M.A./Reading Specialist

Published by ABDO Publishing Company
8000 West 78th Street, Edina, Minnesota 55439.

Printed in the United States.

Editor: Pam Price
Content Developer: Nancy Tuminelly
Cover and Interior Design and Production:
   Anders Hanson, Mighty Media
Illustrations: Bob Doucet
Photo Credits: Shutterstock

Library of Congress Cataloging-in-Publication Data

Scheunemann, Pam, 1955-
  Jumping Jack Russell terriers / Pam Scheunemann ;
illustrator, Bob Doucet.
    p. cm. -- (Dog daze)
  ISBN 978-1-60453-617-1
  1. Jack Russell terrier--Juvenile literature. I. Title.

SF429.J27S34 2009
636.755--dc22
                              2008037964

Super SandCastle™ books are created by a team of
professional educators, reading specialists, and content
developers around five essential components—phonemic
awareness, phonics, vocabulary, text comprehension, and
fluency—to assist young readers as they develop reading
skills and strategies and increase their general
knowledge. All books are written, reviewed, and leveled
for guided reading, early reading intervention, and
Accelerated Reader® programs for use in shared, guided,
and independent reading and writing activities to support
a balanced approach to literacy instruction.

CONTENTS

The
JACK RUSSELL TERRIER

The Jack Russell terrier is a dog that has lots of energy. Jack Russell terriers are small and mostly white. They may have brown or black spots.

Bred for hunting, Jack Russell terriers are smart, athletic, and fearless. They get bored easily. They need lots of exercise and attention.

FACIAL FEATURES

Head

Jack Russell terriers have heads that are wide at the ears and narrow toward the nose.

Teeth and Mouth

Jack Russell terriers have strong jaws. Their top teeth **overlap** the bottom teeth.

Eyes

The eyes of the Jack Russell terrier are dark in color. They are almond shaped.

Ears

Jack Russells have V-shaped ears. Their ears bend toward the front of their heads.

4

BODY BASICS

Size

Jack Russells are usually 10 to 15 inches (25 to 38 cm) tall. They weigh about 16 pounds (7 kg).

Build

Jack Russell terriers are small and sturdy. They are **bred** to hunt.

Tail

The tail of the Jack Russell terrier is about 4 inches (10 cm) long. It stands upright.

Legs and Feet

The legs of Jack Russells are strong and **muscular**. Their feet are round with hard padding.

COAT & COLOR

Jack Russell Terrier Fur

Jack Russell terriers have an inner coat and an outer coat. The inner coat is soft and warm. The outer coat can be smooth, rough, or broken. A broken coat is smooth in some places and rough in others.

White is the main color on a Jack Russell terrier. This color makes it easy for hunters to see the dogs in the woods. They can be all white or have some black, brown, or tan markings.

WHITE FUR

ROUGH COAT WITH TAN AND BROWN MARKINGS

Jack Russell terriers come in a variety of colors and coats.
The photos on these pages show just a few examples.

TAN FUR

BLACK FUR

BROWN FUR

BROKEN COAT WITH
TAN MARKINGS

SMOOTH COAT WITH BLACK
AND TAN MARKINGS

SMOOTH COAT WITH BROWN,
TAN, AND BLACK MARKINGS

HEALTH & CARE

Life Span

The **life span** of the Jack Russell terrier is 13 to 15 years.

Grooming

Jack Russell terriers should be brushed regularly. Their toenails should be clipped often.

The Jack Russell **sheds** throughout the year. Brushing helps limit shedding.

VET'S CHECKLIST

- Have your Jack Russell terrier spayed or neutered.

- Visit a vet for regular checkups.

- Ask your vet which foods are right for your Jack Russell terrier.

- Clean your Jack Russell terrier's teeth and ears once a week.

- Make sure your Jack Russell gets lots of exercise.

- Do not let your Jack Russell terrier overeat.

EXERCISE & TRAINING

Activity Level

Jack Russell terriers are very high-energy dogs. They need a lot of exercise. It is good to let them run outside if you have a fenced-in area. Have plenty of toys for them indoors.

Obedience

A Jack Russell acts like a big dog in a little dog's body. They are determined and willful. Since they were **bred** for hunting, they are often **aggressive**. Obedience training teaches them about good behavior.

A Few Things You'll Need

A **leash** lets your Jack Russell know that you are the boss. With a leash, you can guide your dog where you want it to go. Most cities require that dogs be on leashes when they are outside.

A **collar** is a strap that goes around your Jack Russell's neck. You can attach a leash to the collar to take your dog on walks. You should also attach an **identification tag** with your home address. If your dog ever gets lost, people will know where it lives.

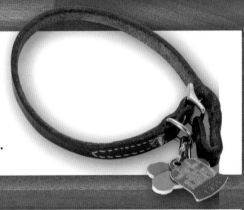

Toys keep your Jack Russell healthy and happy. Dogs like to chase and chew on them.

A **dog bed** will help your pet feel safe and comfortable at night.

ATTITUDE & INTELLIGENCE

Personality

The Jack Russell terrier is lively and **loyal**. It is fearless and curious.

Intellect

The Jack Russell terrier is intelligent and stubborn. It will not back down easily.

All About Me

Hi! My name is Jiffy. I'm a Jack Russell terrier. I just wanted to let you know a few things about me. I made some lists below of things I like and dislike.

Things I Like

- Lots of exercise
- Being trained
- Playing fetch
- Digging holes
- Going for long walks
- Hunting

Things I Dislike

- Being ignored
- Being left alone
- Other pets
- Long toenails

LITTERS & PUPPIES

Litter Size

Female Jack Russell terriers usually give birth to four to eight puppies.

Diet

Newborn pups drink their mother's milk. They can begin to eat soft puppy food when they are about four weeks old.

Growth

They should stay with their mothers until they are eight weeks old. Jack Russell terrier puppies grow until they are about one year old.

BUYING A JACK RUSSELL TERRIER

Choosing a Breeder

It's best to buy a puppy from a **breeder**, not a pet store. When you visit a dog breeder, ask to see the mother and father of the puppies. Make sure the parents are healthy, friendly, and well behaved.

Picking a Puppy

Choose a puppy that isn't too **aggressive** or too shy. If you crouch down, some of the puppies may want to play with you. One of them might be the right one for you!

Is It the Right Dog for You?

Buying a dog is a big decision. You'll want to make sure your new pet suits your lifestyle.

Get out a piece of paper. Draw a line down the middle.

Read the statements listed here. Each time you agree with a statement from the left column, make a mark on the left side of your paper. When you agree with a statement from the right column, make a mark on the right side of your paper.

I like to play with my dog.	☐	☐	I want my dog to entertain itself.
I want to work on training my dog.	☐	☐	I don't have the time to train my dog.
I don't have any other small pets.	☐	☐	I have other small pets.
I spend a lot of time at home.	☐	☐	I'm not home very often.
I like to take my dog with me wherever I go.	☐	☐	I prefer to leave my dog at home.
I like to go for long walks with my dog.	☐	☐	I don't like to exercise with my dog.
I've had other dogs as pets.	☐	☐	I have never had a dog before.
I enjoy an active dog.	☐	☐	I want a lapdog.

If you made more marks on the left side than on the right side, a Jack Russell may be the right dog for you! If you made more marks on the right side of your paper, you might want to consider another breed.

THE FOX HUNTER

John "Jack" Russell was a **parson** who lived in England in the 1800s. He loved fox hunting. And he loved dogs, especially fox terriers. While at Oxford University, Russell bought a small, white-and-tan female terrier that he named Trump. Trump inspired him to start **breeding** small hunting dogs.

Russell wanted to **breed** dogs that had the endurance, speed, and ability to find and hold foxes. The dogs had to be small too, so they could fit into foxholes! After Russell's death, these trusty working dogs became known as Jack Russell terriers.

Tails of Lore
THE ART DOG

Sometimes an animal just stands out from the crowd.
One such animal is Tillamook Cheddar, a Jack Russell
terrier from Brooklyn, New York. Tillie, as her
friends call her, is a true artist who
makes her art from scratch!

Tillie works on a special canvas that captures the impressions she makes with her claws, teeth, and tongue. When her helpers remove the top layer of Tillie's special canvas, her designs are revealed! Tillie has been exhibiting her art in galleries in the United States and Europe since 1999. And in 2005, she gave birth to six healthy puppies!

FIND THE JACK RUSSELL TERRIER

A   B   C   D

THE JACK RUSSELL TERRIER QUIZ

1. Jack Russell terriers are large dogs. True or false?

2. Jack Russell terriers are mostly black. True or false?

3. Some Jack Russell terriers have broken coats. True or false?

4. The life span of a Jack Russell terrier is 17 to 20 years. True or false?

5. Jack Russell terriers need lots of exercise. True or false?

6. A female Jack Russell usually gives birth to four to eight puppies. True or false?

GLOSSARY

aggressive – likely to attack or confront.

breed – 1) a group of animals or plants with common ancestors. 2) to raise animals, such as dogs or cats, that have certain traits. A *breeder* is someone whose job is to breed animals or plants.

life span – the average length of time someone or something exists.

loyal – faithful or devoted to someone or something.

muscular – having well-developed muscles.

overlap – to cover and extend past something.

parson – a minister.

shed – to lose something, such as skin, leaves, or fur, through a natural process.